PRAISE FOR JACQUELINE PIRTLE

Jacqueline takes you always directly to what you are ready to see or experience.

— LONGTIME CLIENT AND READER

It is liberating to face your own blocks and to be finally free of the weight that they have caused for many years. And while for me the changes I'm experiencing are noticeable and real, I still feel like myself. Just a more sure self.

— LONGTIME CLIENT AND READER

Jacqueline makes me BELIEVE I can be and live a joyful and magical existence every new day of my life!

— LONGTIME CLIENT AND READER

The *365 Days of Happiness* bestselling author

JACQUELINE PIRTLE

To BE and Live

The reason you are here!

COPYRIGHT

Copyright © 2021 Jacqueline Pirtle
www.FreakyHealer.com

All rights reserved. No part of this book may be reproduced or transmitted in any form or by any means, electronic or mechanical, including photocopying, recording, or by any information storage and retrieval system without the written permission of the publisher, except where permitted by law.

ISBN-13: 978-1-955059-11-4

Publisher: Freaky Healer

Editor-in-chief: Zoe Pirtle
All-round Support: Mitch Pirtle

Book cover design by Kingwood Creations kingwoodcreations.com

Author photo courtesy of Lionel Madiou madious.com

I want to let you know that all my books and holistic practitioner work together are a wholesome system, supporting you to live a more conscious, mindful, and happier life.

However, I made it so you can receive the benefit of living more joyously solely by working through this terrific journal book, while also experiencing the full satisfaction in continuing on to the next journal of this series—not to mention the rock solid tools you get by reading any of my other books or adding in my podcast *The Daily Freak*. Either way, I know you'll love my inspirational teachings.

Find out more:
www.freakyhealer.com
Amazon Author Page
The Daily Freak Podcast

So before you dive in, I want to thank you for hopping on the magic train with me! I truly hope you enjoy *To BE and Live* as much as I loved writing it, and if you do, it would be wonderful if you could take a short minute and leave a review on Amazon.com and Goodreads.com as soon as you can.

Your kind feedback helps other readers find my books easier, and be happy faster. Consider it a happy deed for the world.

Thank you!

ACKNOWLEDGMENTS

Let's be honest here... I have a dream team!

I could not have finished this book without the help of talented, creative, high-for-life, and phenomenal professionals.

From the bottom of my heart, I want to thank Zoe Pirtle for her editorial mastery; Mitch Pirtle for his all-round support; kingwoodcreations.com for their fun and polished book cover design; and madiouART.com for an amazing photo shoot.

I'd also like to extend a huge "Thank You!" to all fans of my work and books—I created this beautiful journal series for you.

Life is spectacular with you on my side!

*What are you waiting for?
Go BE and live!*

DEDICATION

*I dedicate this journal to all those that dream to **BE and live** more and challenge them to claim their **more** boldly!*

INTRODUCTION

Incredible *BE-er and live-er*,

I always open my books with how happy I am to be a part in someone's journey, so I'll stick with that because it never gets old and it's the truth.

Thank you for including me in your life by reading and working through my journal *To BE and Live*!

To **BE and live** is something I say often in my work, podcast, and all of my books—and now I have even created a journal about it, so let me explain:

With **BE**, I mean existing as your whole being - your body, mind, soul, and your consciousness - and how you show up as such.

With **live**, I mean how you are experiencing and animating your physical life.

High-for-life is something else that I mention all the time. It is a state where you are aligned with your truc you, your well-feeling, and your happiness—whatever that might be and no matter the circumstances. Nothing can inspire you to be anyone or anything else than yourself when you are in your high-for-life

INTRODUCTION

frequency. It is a state of constant change and a deeply, securely, rooted-as-yourself way of being and living.

Everything is energy - you, me, this journal, and all of life - it's all *ONE* and the same: Energy! It's also all connected and sharing at all times—meaning that you living your life through the deeper ways that you are creating in this journal will spread to everything and everyone. That's really appreciated all around the globe, so thank you for that!

As these energies, everything and everyone vibrates in different frequencies—some are high like happiness and feeling beautiful, while others are lower like frustration or feeling insecure.

But no worries my dear journaler, you will definitely be in the higher frequency with the work you are about to embark on. The clear intention of this journal *To BE and Live*!

While it's important to embrace all parts of life that are making this casserole of "different" a wonderful entity, it is in your best interest to use your natural power and shift things to match your wishes, or change your perception so you can love your life.

It's easy to get sidetracked walking through your time busily while being in the midst of all, because in such a state of multitasking forgetting why you're really here is a natural balancing act—shutting one part off because the other is too much. But it's also a sort of cry for help since your focus is not aligned with your inner being and your reasons to exist.

The solution is not to stop life altogether or tone down what you are experiencing; instead, it's a shift of focus onto what matters and to remember that fully.

That's why your work in this journal is so important, because it helps you to pull yourself back into the basic meanings of why you are alive—to not have this cry turn into something bigger or deeper.

Think of this journal as a lasso that catches you, then guides you to re-focus on your true values and reasons to BE and live so you can truly connect and hear your inner being—making your life an experience you love. That shift to magic can be achieved by focusing on a page a day to revive your foundational reasons for being alive every split second.

To BE and Live helps you find your way home to your soul being so you can step into your unlimited-ness—entering a space of alignment, power, health, success, abundance, and happiness. There, an ocean of opportunities will catch hold of you, inviting you to latch on. Just think of that incredible match-up, and shift into the higher frequency of bliss by being *ONE* with the excitement of these manifestations.

It's a true act of giving magic the stage of momentum, and of being and living the best version of you—while changing at a constant and vivid speed, the way life naturally happens.

Journaling through this 30 day journal of *To BE and Live* brings huge eye-opening moments to the table so that you can be and live like you never have before, craft a life beyond your dreams, and re-discover your truest reasons, desires, and feelings. So much so, that you will become a master in feeling phenomenal and manifesting what you want—all while learning to go for it and live more consciously and mindfully, a change that is forever!

As a side note, there are a couple bonus days at the end in case you ever find the need to do two in a day, or to keep working while you wait for the next journal in this series to arrive. I also left you a few blank to **BE and live** pages to journal about deepening your joy for being alive.

Enough chit-chat, I know you are ready, so grab your pen and have incredible fun with catching more life than you have ever caught, in your new crazy ways.

Happiest,
    Jacqueline

 Day 1

IMAGINE you have a light that is yours to shine bright and in order to light it, in case it's not lit, or make it brighter - if it's a bit dimmed - you close your eyes and visualize a beautiful lantern with a glorious candle in the middle of your heart space. Visualize this heart-touching sight for a while, and breathe into this enlightening event! When ready, open up your lantern and take your candle into your hands. Spend some time here by graciously admiring its beauty! Then, take a match and light your candle—sense the magic in this action, the warmth of this happening, and witness your light getting bigger and bigger to shine brighter and brighter. Time to put your light back into your heart space, your lantern, and close it to have it stay lit forever and ever—it's your birthright! How does it feel to BE and live your light so truly bright?

_____
_____
_____
_____
_____
_____
_____
_____
_____
_____
_____
_____
_____

To BE and Live - The reason you are here!

ay 2

Now that your light is so bright, what does to *BE* even mean for you? Seriously, how do you feel when you are in a pure state of being—where all you have is your breath, when all you are is your breath, and when all that's happening is your breathing? Close your eyes and sit with this for a little! Feel yourself being, and lose yourself in your beautiful nothing space of pure light. The following lines are your space to shine! Go on, BE!

___

To BE and Live - The reason you are here!

ay 3

AS YOUR SHINING LIGHT, what do the following words bring up for you: To *live*! Go Live! Do life! Live fully and vividly! Don't hold back! Go all out! What feelings, imaginations, visualizations, thoughts, ideas, inspirations, realizations, plans, shifts, permissions, or changes are coming in? I'm pushing you to go magnificent here!

_____
_____
_____
_____
_____
_____
_____
_____
_____
_____
_____
_____
_____
_____
_____
_____
_____
_____
_____

To BE and Live - The reason you are here!

 ay 4

Now comes the fun part! Put *Day 2* and *Day 3* together and write about what your *right now* reasons to BE and live are! Then keep coming back to add more, and more, and even more glorious reasons as you go on in this journal. Let this entry grow! You are a true super be-er and live-er!

_____
_____
_____
_____
_____
_____
_____
_____
_____
_____
_____
_____
_____
_____
_____
_____
_____
_____
_____
_____
_____
_____
_____
_____

To BE and Live - The reason you are here!

Day 5

BRAVO! You now have your own marching orders! How much cooler can it get? What are you going to focus on, so you will actually BE and live the most happiest ever today? What feelings, thoughts, words, activities, food and drinks, clothes, or intentions are a match to your bliss-plan?

_____
_____
_____
_____
_____
_____
_____
_____
_____
_____
_____
_____
_____
_____
_____
_____
_____
_____
_____
_____

To BE and Live - The reason you are here!

 ay 6

WHEN WAS the last time you took a path of adventure—either as your physical you or in your imagination? Go on, what kind of stunt can you pull off to feel excited? Even better, choose two; one in physicality, like a new hiking trail, a wild dance, or a fun trip; and one in imagination—flying a dragon sounds like a real winner here.

_____
_____
_____
_____
_____
_____
_____
_____
_____
_____
_____
_____
_____
_____
_____
_____
_____
_____
_____
_____

To BE and Live - The reason you are here!

 Day 7

Your powerful love is the purity of being and living—and by sensing into this incredible essence you will feel amazing. How will you feel your own love more vividly? What heart-touching happenings can you create to nourish your love?

___

To BE and Live - The reason you are here!

 Day 8

ON A PHYSICAL LEVEL, as your body in life, what types of practices can you come up with to bring some spice and wonder into your experience of aliveness to enrich your way of being and living? As an idea and example, sitting by a stream is wonderful for your physical body while also deeply nourishing for *being*. Taking in nature is a guaranteed magic pill for joy! What exercise is right for you?

_____
_____
_____
_____
_____
_____
_____
_____
_____
_____
_____
_____
_____
_____
_____
_____
_____
_____
_____

To BE and Live - The reason you are here!

 ay 9

Do you think a singing bird, a waterfall, splashing waves, a basketball bouncing, a motorcycle making a bunch of noise, children laughing loudly, tears in someone's eyes or bliss in another's smile, a future loved one's first "nice to meet you" and a loved one's last "goodbye" are rich in aliveness and life itself? Definitely! That means it's easy to create, notice, and latch onto a lot more of being and living *vivid*ly in your everyday existence— since these are everyday happenings. Go on, journal about this always present vividness!

___

To BE and Live - The reason you are here!

 ay 10

To BE and live means you will eat yummy, delicious, and fitting food. What will that be for you today, and then every day after? How can you let go of old unfitting food rules and make it healthier for you? In case you desire to indulge into something a little extra, how can you feel good about your treat by tasting its aliveness? Managing to align with its sweet energy means you shift to that sweetness too—and when in such great sync, your digestion will function wonderfully. Here is a great example: tuning into the high-for-life, sweet, and soft energy of cotton candy means that you fill every single cell of your whole being with that well-feeling essence. Fun fact—that shift happens if you end up eating it or decide only to align with it.

___

To BE and Live - The reason you are here!

 ay 11

CHOOSING a happy life is in direct alignment with what you came here to experience! Of course, sometimes the opposite is present so you learn the difference between your own unique happiness and un-happiness, but suffering and feeling unwell is not meant to be your constant state. How will you stay true to your original reasons to be alive, to who you really are, and to what you truly want—which is a wonderful life? What bliss, satisfaction, cheerfulness, and merriment will you give yourself today, tomorrow, and every day after?

_____

To BE and Live - The reason you are here!

 ay 12

THERE ARE multiple dimensions of you being and living your life. Two of these levels are your physicality and your energetic essence. The physical can be enhanced by giving your best in life, while the energetic is nourished by you listening to your inner voice that seems crazy and unexplainable at times. What does it mean for you, to give yourself the best in life? How will you follow your gut instinct more often—and how willing are you to trust it unconditionally?

_____
_____
_____
_____
_____
_____
_____
_____
_____
_____
_____
_____
_____
_____
_____
_____
_____
_____
_____

To BE and Live - The reason you are here!

Day 13

REALIZING that making yourself number one is for your own good when it comes to living your life, is key to experiencing your deeply engraved soul passion and soul journey. Focusing on your health, success, abundance, and happiness while aligning with your soul being - which is always connected and *ONE* with consciousness - is the trick to staying true to who you really are. Best thing is that, as such, you will serve the whole world since you are always sharing and spreading the *what* and *who* that you are. So how will you make yourself your own number one permanently?

_____
_____
_____
_____
_____
_____
_____
_____
_____
_____
_____
_____
_____
_____
_____
_____

To BE and Live - The reason you are here!

ay 14

Your heart is always immensely involved in you being alive—not just physically, but also as a factory of your love, and the host of your inner being filled with unlimited wisdom. How will you honor your heart physically? Maybe with exercise, or with better food for your heart? How can you show grace for your heart emotionally, in thoughts, and energetically? How will you align with your pure positive vessel more often?

To BE and Live - The reason you are here!

 ay 15

Change is an amazing way out, forward, left, or right, alongside being the natural way to BE and live your life. Change also screams adventure, excitement, expansion, and a calibration into a higher YOU—which is the case even if you do not feel it as a good thing. How can you create more thrilling change? Would a new ice cream flavor do the trick here? What kind of change are you desperately wishing for? What kind of change do you not love and how can you get in sync with it?

___

To BE and Live - The reason you are here!

 ay 16

A LOWER FREQUENCY lifestyle filled with problems, anger, or negativity is always available and possible if you choose to focus on that. But who's really into such a thing? What's your determined high-for-life tactic to stay positive—and through that, choosing to create a life that you love?

___

To BE and Live - The reason you are here!

 ay 17

IMAGINE yourself living vividly while focusing on being in your NOW! That right there is an invitation for life to deliver your wishes and dreams without any hesitation, reason being that life is vivid and in the NOW, making you the perfect match to life's frequency—versus a not lifelike existence, living dull and in the past, which slows the arrival of magic down. How will you bring more vividness to the table? What is your "I shall focus on my NOW" alarm?

To BE and Live - The reason you are here!

 ay 18

WHEN THINKING about the purest way of being and living, a flowing, relaxed, lighthearted, happy, fulfilled, unstoppable, and powerful energy is present. Sense this, breathe into it, and write about how this feels for you. Now go into your physical body. Where do you feel anything less than this well-feeling? Is there any kind of pain or an ache somewhere? Find it, focus on it, then breathe the well-feeling energy you wrote about into that spot—notice the healing shift happening. Repeat this practice with your thoughts and emotions—detect them and breathe this wellness into them. How do you feel now? Use this exercise whenever needed.

To BE and Live - The reason you are here!

Day 19

FEELINGS ARE a great replacement for a rollercoaster ride if you physically can't hop on one! I imagine this giving you a giggle but all joking aside, how can you flow in your ups and downs, and lefts and rights, of your feelings more smoothly—like you would on a fun ride? How can you embrace all of your emotions without resisting? Is accepting, respecting, appreciating, thanking, and loving them a possibility? I truly hope so!

To BE and Live - The reason you are here!

 ay 20

To BE and live fully means you have to go for what is in life by letting it happen. When was the last time you went for whatever the *it* was by taking the invitation? What will it take for you to go skydiving, eat that most spicy pepper, dance like you have never danced before, laugh until you pee in your pants, love open-heartedly, or feel over the moon magical? The Universe says "I got you," your life says "Go for it!"—and all you need to say is, "Yes!" Now the question is, yes to what?

To BE and Live - The reason you are here!

 Day 21

OLD AND UNFITTING habits and beliefs have no space in being, and living fully and vividly—hence, being in deep meadows of gunk does not feel good. What old stuff will you wave good bye to? Which old habits and thoughts will you send the intention of "Good riddance!" to? Maybe choreograph a happy dance to help this along!

To BE and Live - The reason you are here!

ay 22

To have a great life you must let everyone else have a great life too! Being one-sided won't do here. Gossiping, judging, negativing, holding non-budging expectations of others, or asking them to change for you creates huge roadblocks on your path to happiness and to live the best life ever, creating unwell-feeling energy for you and everyone involved—whereas respecting everything and everyone as-is allows unlimited light for all. How will you be the light-creator of your time?

To BE and Live - The reason you are here!

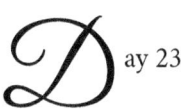 ay 23

To BE and live up to date with what is right, fitting, and well feeling for you, a flowing mind willing to change with your ever modernizing inner being is of the utmost importance. With what or whom are you standing still in a rusty old way going nowhere? How can you change, and instead, go with the modern you? Go on, let it flow!

To BE and Live - The reason you are here!

Day 24

LIVING your strength - physically and energetically, emotionally, thoughtfully, soulfully, and consciously - brings on a powerful way of being and living. What kind of vision pops into your mind when you focus on your strong whole being, living a strong life, while being one with a strong Universe? Go all tough here—you might even want to flex your muscles a bit!

To BE and Live - The reason you are here!

 ay 25

ALL TYPES of love in physical life belong to a life fully lived! There is self love which is crucial to being happy, love for others as a wonderful co-creation, love for nature which is highly nourishing, and the love for life itself. So much love—not to forget love of chocolate! What is love for you? How do you experience love—who and what do you love? How does it feel? Be really loving here, and then carry your love - and let love carry you - wherever you go.

___

To BE and Live - The reason you are here!

 ay 26

LIFE IS a fantastic mix of everything; beauty, peace, success, abundance, colors, regal-ness, graciousness, love, light, happiness, and joy—but also of all the opposites of these high-for-life essences. What are you going to do about those opposites in order to BE and live a terrific life regardless?

To BE and Live - The reason you are here!

# Day 27

LIVING life serves you plenty of moments to lick your wounds! How you treat your symptoms - physically and energetically, emotionally, thoughtfully, and consciously - makes all the difference. So how do you treat your aches and pains, or your tears and distress—gracefully? How will you unconditionally love all parts of you, even if they seem like trouble? And how can you scoop up all the wisdom sitting in the middle of all your issues?

To BE and Live - The reason you are here!

 ay 28

BOLDNESS IS life's elixir of alignment with who you really are. Why? Because it nourishes your fearlessly gigantic energetic essence that you naturally are, alongside making your light shine bright so you can show it off to the world. Being courageous also saves lives—at least in some situations. When coming into physicality, you said that you will dashingly be YOU and it's about high time to make that your full reality. How can you show up boldly, or even bolder that you are now? What will you newly do, say, stand for, or act on while being so daring?

___

To BE and Live - The reason you are here!

# Day 29

CAN we agree that little - or big - signs are always present in life for you to clearly notice? What do you do when these messages show themselves? Do you follow them, and do you consciously tune into them? How much wisdom do you sense in their appearances? How can you notice these messages more often and allow this always available information? Sitting still to see them, chit-chatting and squeezing all of that golden guidance out of them, or laughing with them, are all great options and examples.

To BE and Live - The reason you are here!

ay 30

You have read, thought of, and written about many processes in this journal, and you have gotten truer and wilder in your ways of being and living as YOU. Question is, how much grander and happier can you BE and live? Definitely more, since there is never a limit! What does your *more* look like? What and who is included in it? How will you dance, speak, feel, celebrate, and most importantly, BE and live more?

_____
_____
_____
_____
_____
_____
_____
_____
_____
_____
_____
_____
_____
_____
_____

To BE and Live - The reason you are here!

* * *

Ready to continue on your self-growth path? Get the next journal in this series: ***High for Life: The best case scenario!***

BONUS

Because hey, nobody ever wants the goodness to end.

Keep on being and living like you never have before!

 ay 31

RELAXING IS WORTH GOLD, unless you order an already stressed person to relax immediately. That never works! So let's make sure that you are not even going into the vicinity of being stressed, so that when it's time to relax, you actually can. First, sense into your whole being—how are you feeling? Next, list all your little and big stresses while imagining that once they hit the paper, they stay on the paper, at least for now! Then, breathe into this beautiful nothing space you just created for yourself. Ask, "How will I allow more relaxation so I can enjoy my life fully and vividly?" And lastly, if you still would like to, pick up your stress points again—but now, carry them with ease.

___

To BE and Live - The reason you are here!

 Day 32

KNOWING ALL that you know now - about yourself and your life - and feeling everything clearer than before, how much more truth in being and living will you create for yourself? How strong is your will to make it a priority? What crazy-ness do you have in mind? Will it involve a wild run through the forest? You might laugh, but hey, why not?

___

To BE and Live - The reason you are here!

 ay 33

BEING and living high-for-life is a state of magnificence—one that represents colorful happiness and pure bliss even when life takes you on a horror ride. Sounds dramatic, I know—but it was too tempting not to use. Nowhere is it written that you have to love anything that is giving you trouble, ever! But in order to enjoy a masterful life up to your highest standards, it's helpful to look at everything as a gift, on the other end of its gunk—meaning, you deal with your lumps of coal through being in your high-for-life frequency. There, they usually turn out to be diamonds. What trouble comes to mind, and how will you harvest its magic?

_____
_____
_____
_____
_____
_____
_____
_____
_____
_____
_____
_____
_____
_____
_____
_____

To BE and Live - The reason you are here!

Day 34

THIS ONE ENTRY always has a special place in my journals by pointing out a different angle with each different one. So let's go! Nay-sayers, negative-ers, and down-ers are not deeply embedded in being and living a life to its full magical extent—probably not even half actually. So why even give their lower essence your precious time by going low too? Why not instead shower them with your bright light—and keep going in your aligned path to BE and live? How will you persistently do such a high frequency act?

___

To BE and Live - The reason you are here!

Day 35

IMAGINE BEING a professional BE-er and Live-er—one that is alive and ticking. One that chose to come into physicality, breathes automatically, feels, hears, tastes and smells, thinks, and sees just like like that. One that laughs and cries all through life and eats food because of being alive—well, and also because it tastes good. Think of a lucky person like that! I know quite a few —and one of them is you. How lucky are you really? How well trained are you in being your BE-er and Live-er? Please tell me that you are having fun with this!

To BE and Live - The reason you are here!

AND NOW IT'S YOUR TURN!

The following are your magical pages to shift your being and living even higher.

I'm counting on you to go all vivid here!

 ay 36

TO BE AND LIVE MEANS...

To BE and Live - The reason you are here!

 Day 37

TO BE AND LIVE MEANS…

To BE and Live - The reason you are here!

Day 38

TO BE AND LIVE MEANS…

To BE and Live - The reason you are here!

Day 39

TO BE AND LIVE MEANS...

___

To BE and Live - The reason you are here!

ay 40

TO BE AND LIVE MEANS...

_____
_____
_____
_____
_____
_____
_____
_____
_____
_____
_____
_____
_____
_____
_____
_____
_____
_____
_____
_____
_____

To BE and Live - The reason you are here!

* * *

Don't forget to leave a review on Amazon.com and Goodreads.com as soon as you can, as your kind feedback helps other readers find my books easier. Thank you!

ALSO BY JACQUELINE PIRTLE

365 Days of Happiness

Because happiness is a piece of cake!

This passage book invites you to create a daily habit to live your every day joy, and is the parent companion to *365 Days of Happiness*, the journal workbook.

* * *

365 Days of Happiness - Special Edition

Because happiness is a piece of cake

This beautiful Special Edition of the bestseller *365 Days of Happiness: Because happiness is a piece of cake* has room for your notes after every daily passage.

* * *

365 Days of Happiness - Journal Workbook

Because happiness is a piece of cake

This enlightening journal workbook is your daily tool to create a habit of living your every day bliss, and is the companion to *365 Days of Happiness: Because happiness is a piece of cake*.

* * *

Life IS Beautiful

Here's to New Beginnings

If you like digging deeper into the meaning of life and are inspired by spirituality, then you'll love Jacqueline's effective teachings.

* * *

Parenting Through the Eyes of Lollipops

A Guide to Conscious Parenting

If you like harmony at home and laughter in the house, then you'll love Jacqueline's inspirational methods.

* * *

What it Means to BE a Woman

And Yes! Women do Poop!

If you like to live free, empowered, and want to decide for yourself, then you'll love Jacqueline's liberating ways.

* * *

What. If. - Turning your what IFs into it IS!

A 30 Day or 90 Day - Extended Edition - Journal

If you like to be in charge of your own life, turn your dreams into reality, enjoy journaling, and want to squeeze the most out of your time, then you'll love Jacqueline uplifting teachings.

* * *

Open - Where it all starts!

A 30 Day or 90 Day - Extended Edition - Journal

If you like to be open to live your life fully, allow your dreams to come true, enjoy journaling, and want to squeeze the most out of your time, then you'll love Jacqueline Pirtle's uplifting teachings.

ABOUT THE AUTHOR

Bestselling author, podcaster, and holistic practitioner, Jacqueline Pirtle, has twenty-four years of experience helping thousands of clients discover their own happiness. Jacqueline is the owner of *FreakyHealer* and has shared her solid teachings through her podcast **The Daily Freak**, sessions, workshops, presentations, and books with clients all over the world. She holds international degrees in holistic health and natural living. Her effective healing work has been featured in print and online magazines, podcasts, radio shows, on TV, and in the documentary *The Overly Emotional Child by Learning Success*, available on Amazon Prime.

For any questions you might have, to sign up for Jacqueline's newsletter, and for more information on whatever else she is up to, visit www.freakyhealer.com and her social media accounts @freakyhealer.

www.ingramcontent.com/pod-product-compliance
Lightning Source LLC
Chambersburg PA
CBHW071423070526
44578CB00003B/675